hrjc

Variation in Living Things

Robert Snedden

Chicago, Illinois

www.capstonepub.com
Visit our website to find out more information about Heinemann-Raintree books.

To order:

☎ Phone 888-454-2279

🖥 Visit www.capstonepub.com to browse our catalog and order online.

Edited by Andrew Farrow, Adrian Vigliano, and Diyan Leake
Designed by Victoria Allen
Picture research by Elizabeth Alexander
Illustrations by Oxford Designers & Illustrators
Originated by Capstone Global Library Ltd
Printed and bound in China by South China Printing Company Ltd

15 14 13 12 11
10 9 8 7 6 5 4 3 2 1

Library of Congress Cataloging-in-Publication Data
Snedden, Robert.

Variation in living things / Robert Snedden.—1st ed.

p. cm.—(The web of life)

Includes bibliographical references and index.

ISBN 978-1-4109-4400-9 (hb (freestyle))—ISBN 978-1-4109-4407-8 (pb (freestyle)) 1. Variation (Biology)—Juvenile literature. I. Title.

QH401.S56 2012

576.5′4—dc23   2011017721

Acknowledgements
The author and publisher are grateful to the following for permission to reproduce copyright material: Corbis p. 27 (© Brian J. Skerry/National Geographic Society); Getty Images p. 41 (Evaristo SA/AFP); Moorfields communications team p. 39; Photolibrary pp. 5 (momentimages), 7 (Johann Schumacher), 10 (Javier Larrea), 13 (Dennis Kunkel), 28 (Gilles Martin), 29 (Bildagentur RM), 33 (Roger Eritja), 37 (Pixmann Limited), 40 (Gary k Smith); Press Association Images p. 6 (Troy Maben); Science Photo Library p. 20 (Oak Ridge National Laboratory / US Department Of Energy), 23 (Juergen Berger), 22 (Eye of Science), 38 (Philippe Plailly/Eurelios; Shutterstock pp. 9 (© Mateusz Kopyt), 12 (© Katie Smith Photography), 17 (© Francois van Heerden), 14 (© Eduard Kyslynskyy), 19 top (© aguilarphoto), 19 bottom (© Denise Kappa), 21 (© HelleM), 24 (© r.nagy), 30 (© Malota), 34 (© Jan Hopgood), 35 (© FotoVeto), 36 (© Ron Hilton), 18 (© Linda Bucklin), 43 (© Valentyn Volkov), 43 (© Dulce Rubia), 43 (© Monticello), 42 (© Africa Studio), 42 (© Awardimages), 42 (© Zloneg), 42 (© matin), 43 (© Petr Malyshev), 43 (© Piotr Malczyk).

Cover photograph of blond (white) and brown grizzly bears playfighting reproduced with permission of Photolibrary (Steven Kazlowski/Peter Arnold Images).

Every effort has been made to contact copyright holders of material reproduced in this book. Any omissions will be rectified in subsequent printings if notice is given to the publisher.

Disclaimer
All the internet addresses (URLs) given in this book were valid at the time of going to press. However, due to the dynamic nature of the internet, some addresses may have changed, or sites may have changed or ceased to exist since publication. While the author and publisher regret any inconvenience this may cause readers, no responsibility for any such changes can be accepted by either the author or the publisher.

Contents

Some words appear in the text in bold, **like this**. You can find out what they mean by looking in the glossary.

The Same–but Different

It is usually easy to see the differences between the various kinds of plants and animals. For example, a penguin looks very different from an owl, and a tomato looks very different from an oak tree. But how different can one owl be from another owl of the same kind? What differences might there be between one tomato plant and another?

Species

Scientists divide the living world into a number of different groupings of **organisms**. Each member of the group shares certain characteristics. For example, birds are a group of animals that all have feathers—a feature found in no other living things. Birds can be divided up into smaller groups, such as owls and penguins.

The smallest division that can be made is the **species**, such as the tawny owl or the king penguin. Members of a species can breed together to produce offspring that will also be able to reproduce themselves. Individual members of a species have many things in common, but they may also be strikingly different.

Variation

The difference between one individual living thing of one species and another of the same species is called variation. Variation applies to all living things, including us. You just have to look at the people around you to see how varied we humans can be.

Differences can matter

Just as some people are taller than others, some birds in a species have slightly longer beaks than others have. The longer beaked birds might find it easier to get insects out of tree bark, which may mean they eat better than the short beaked birds. This advantage could mean that the longer beaked birds are more likely to raise their young successfully.

Some of the rich variety of the human race can be seen here.

A Closer Look at Species

Although we think of a **species** as being the basic unit of the way we classify living things, there is no accurate definition of what a species actually is. It is true that members of the same species can produce **fertile** offspring together, but in some cases members of different but similar species can also mate and produce fertile offspring.

The grolar bear

Grizzly bears are found in North America, ranging from the northwest United States, through western Canada, and into Alaska. In recent years they have been moving farther north and east into areas where polar bears roam. In 2006, the first grolar bear was found—the result of a mating between a male grizzly bear and a female polar bear.

Polar bears and grizzly bears are closely related, but they have always been considered as separate species. The grolar bear is not a new species. It is something called a **hybrid**, which is the result of a cross between two different species. Hybrids are fairly common in nature where the territories of similar species overlap.

This grolar bear had a polar bear mother and a grizzly bear father.

Races

The northern flicker is a type of woodpecker that is found over large areas of North America. There are two distinct varieties of northern flicker. In fact, they are so distinct, that the northern flicker was once thought to be two different species.

In the east, the "yellow-shafted" flicker has distinctive yellow wing feathers. In the west, the "red-shafted" flicker has red wing feathers. Where the two types meet, they interbreed freely, producing young with mixed red and yellow feathers.

This example shows how a species can sometimes be divided into smaller groups. These are called **subspecies** and races. They are different from each other, but they are not different enough to be grouped as separate species. Yellow-shafted and red-shafted flickers look different, but the fact that they breed together so easily shows that they are actually two varieties of the same species.

This bird was once thought to be one of two distinct species (the yellow-shafted flicker and the red-shafted flicker). This one is the yellow-shafted variety of the northern flicker.

Types of variation

There are two types of variation in a species. These are called **continuous variation** and **discontinuous variation**.

Continuous variation

For most variations, the individuals in a population show a range of differences. This is known as continuous variation. Height and weight are examples of continuous variation. If you look at a group of people, such as a group of students in the same grade, they range from the shortest to the tallest, with many possible heights in between.

The bell curve

If you look at a group of people, you will probably see that most are around the same height; only a few are either very short or very tall. If you were to measure everyone and plot their heights on a graph, you would get a bell-shaped curve that is highest in the middle and falls off evenly on either side. It shows how variations are distributed in a normal group.

Number of people

Height

Discontinuous variation

For some types of variation, there are only a few possibilities for each characteristic. One obvious example of this is gender, where an **organism** is usually either male or female. (There are exceptions to this. For example, snails, slugs, and earthworms can be both male and female at the same time.) Another example, which we will look at later, is blood group.

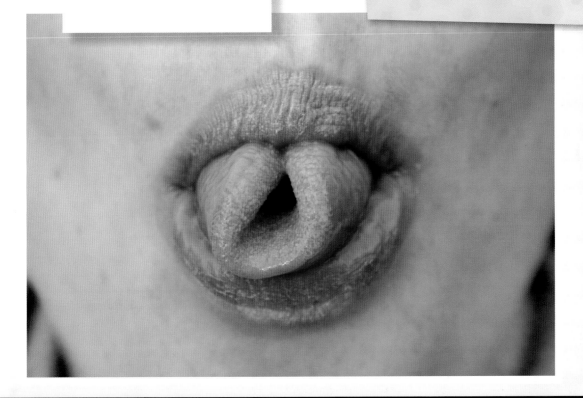

Can you curl your tongue? Some people can, and some can't. This is an example of discontinuous variation.

WORD BANK
continuous variation   variation that takes place over a range of measurements, for example height and weight
discontinuous   variation in which there are only a few distinct varieties, with nothing in between.

Generation to Generation

Living things always develop in a similar way to the parents that produced them. A pig will never give birth to a puppy, a goose won't hatch from a seagull's egg, and an apple tree won't grow from a grass seed. This might seem obvious, but why should it be?

Genes

All living things are made of **cells**, the smallest units of life. Everything began life as a single cell that divided again and again until it became a fully formed **organism**. Each cell contains the information needed to control this process. This information is stored in the cell in the form of **genes**.

You might think of genes as being instructions for the different characteristics that each living thing has. For example, genes control the color of your eyes and the way your body responds to different diseases.

WHAT IT MEANS FOR US

Understanding how genes work has given modern scientists the means to produce crops that have many beneficial characteristics. For instance, crops can have a greater resistance to disease and drought, and greater yield of fruits and seeds. Plants can be grown from single cells in a laboratory, making the process of producing new varieties much faster.

Patterns of inheritance

It was an Austrian monk named Gregor Mendel (1822–1884) who began to make the first discoveries about genes. He studied the way characteristics were passed from one generation of pea plants to the next. From his observations, he described two laws of **heredity**, the process by which genes are passed from one generation to the next:

- His first law says that each characteristic is determined by a separate hereditary unit. We now call them genes. The genes are found in pairs, one coming from the mother and one from the father.

- His second law, which we will explore later, says that different characteristics can be **inherited** independently of one another. For example, a pea plant might be tall with white flowers or short with white flowers. Its height does not affect its flower color.

Today we know that Mendel was right in many respects—but he didn't know the whole story. Several genes acting together control some characteristics, and sometimes characteristics can be linked to each other.

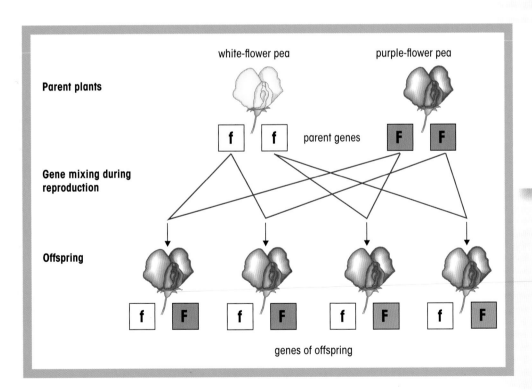

white-flower pea · purple-flower pea

Parent plants

f   f   parent genes   F   F

Gene mixing during reproduction

Offspring

f F   f F   f F   f F

genes of offspring

For each characteristic, one of each pair of genes is inherited from each parent.

Variation and inheritance

You've probably noticed how people sometimes look at children and talk about how much they look like their parents. This is because many of the variations we see in living things are passed on from one generation to the next.

Genetic variation

Each new living thing has features in common with both parents because the genes it has come from them. Yet the new living thing is different from either of its parents because it has a new combination of genes. Whenever **fertilization** takes place, whether in animals or in plants, a unique set of genes is created. This recombining of genes is one of the things that brings about variation.

Common confusions

Are identical twins really identical?

Identical twins used to be regarded as an exception to the rule that no living things have the same genes. Because they developed from a single fertilized egg, it was believed that they would have exactly the same set of genes. Researchers have discovered recently, however, that this isn't quite true. There are some differences, and these can be important. For example, one twin might have leukemia (a type of cancer that affects the blood), while the other doesn't.

Genome

All of the information needed to build and maintain a living organism is coded into its genes. The complete set of genes carried by an organism is called its **genome**. Each member of a species has a very similar genome. The giraffe genome is a set of instructions for making a giraffe, the birch tree genome makes a birch tree, and, of course, the human genome makes a human.

Small differences

From one person to the next, 99.9 percent of the human genome is identical. It is only that 0.1 percent that is different. That 0.1 percent helps to make us all unique individuals.

WHAT IT MEANS FOR US

By mapping the human genome, scientists have made great advances in discovering how differences in our genomes can have a big effect on health. For example, a drug that can help one patient can be harmful to another because of differences in their genes. Statins, used to lower cholesterol, can cause weakening of the muscles in people with a particular gene.

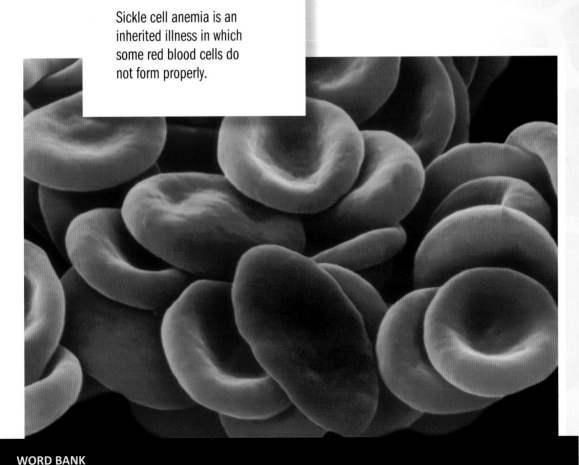

Sickle cell anemia is an inherited illness in which some red blood cells do not form properly.

WORD BANK
fertilization   when a sperm cell joins with an egg to make a new cell with two genomes
genome   all of the genetic information held in the cells of an organism

Dominant and recessive genes

We don't actually have a single genome—we have two. Each of our parents gives us one complete set of genes. When fertilization takes place, a sperm cell (which has one copy of the genome) joins with an egg (which has another copy) to make a new cell with two genomes.

Alleles

The two copies of a particular gene are called **alleles**. The particular combination of alleles found in each individual is another of the factors that helps make us all unique. In one of Mendel's experiments, he crossed pea plants that always had purple flowers with pea plants that always had white flowers. He discovered that all of the plants resulting from this cross had purple flowers.

In the purple-flowered plants, the alleles for flower color were both for purple. In the white-flowered plants, they were both for white. When the plants were crossed, the offspring got one purple allele and one white allele—yet the result was that they were all purple. Why should this be?

The unusual coloring of a white tiger is the result of a recessive gene.

The allele for purple flowers is the one that determines the color of the flowers. It is said to be **dominant** over the allele for white flowers, which is said to be **recessive**. White flowers only appear in plants that have two white alleles. Where there is also a purple allele present, it masks the effect of the white allele.

Genome and genotype

The combined effect of the genomes, determined by which of the alleles is dominant and which recessive, results in the organism's **genotype**. While the genome is all of the organism's genes, the genotype is the actual effect these genes have on the organism's development.

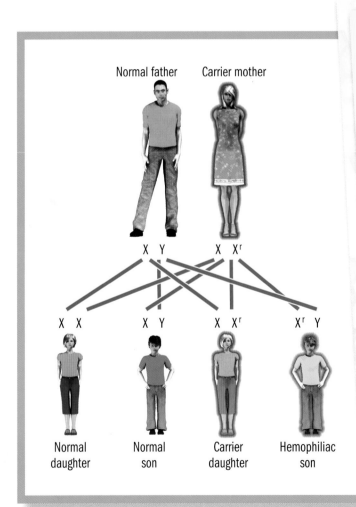

Normal father   Carrier mother

X Y   X X^r

X X   X Y   X X^r X^r Y

Normal daughter   Normal son   Carrier daughter   Hemophiliac son

WHAT IT MEANS FOR US

Dominant and recessive genes can be very important for us, especially where genetic illnesses are concerned. Hemophilia is a disease in which the blood does not clot efficiently. This means that even a small wound can be serious. Hemophilia is caused by a faulty gene. Boys only have one copy of the gene in question, and if it is a faulty one, the disease becomes apparent. Girls are protected by having a dominant working copy of the gene, but they can be carriers of the disease and run the risk of passing it on to their sons.

Independent assortment

In his first experiments with peas, Gregor Mendel was looking at single characteristics, such as whether the flowers were white or purple, whether the seeds were round or wrinkled, or whether the plants were tall or short. Then he began to look at what happened when the parents differed by more than one characteristic—for example, tall plants with purple flowers and short plants with white flowers.

Multiplying differences

It is easier to see what Mendel discovered by looking at a diagram. Capital letters are used to show dominant alleles, and lowercase letters to show recessive alleles. Suppose we have one plant with alleles AABB and another with alleles aabb of the A and B genes. These genes control height (A) and flower color (B). The diagram below shows all of the 16 possible combinations that are possible from just these two genes. As you can see, only one combination produces a short plant with white flowers.

Crossing two characteristics

Key

- alleles from parent 1
- alleles from parent 2
- tall with purple flowers
- tall with white flowers
- short with purple flowers
- short with white flowers

	AB	Ab	aB	ab
AB	AABB	AABb	AaBB	AaBb
Ab	AABb	AAbb	AaBb	AAbb
aB	AaBB	AaBb	aaBB	aaBb
ab	AaBb	AAbb	aaBb	aabb

The more gene pairs we look at, the more the possible combinations start to multiply enormously. For parents differing by 10 genes, there are almost 60,000 possible combinations in their offspring. If there are 20 different pairs, the number jumps to nearly 3.5 billion. Now consider that there are around 20,000 genes in the human genome, and you can begin to see just how unique we all are.

Here we see the variety that just two genes can bring about. The B gene determines eye color (B dominant = brown eyes, b recessive = blue eyes), and the Y gene determines either curly hair (Y dominant) or straight hair (y recessive). So, in this example, a person has to have bbyy genes to have blue eyes and straight hair.

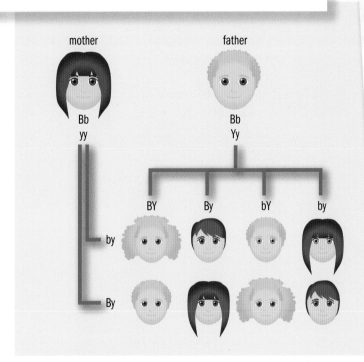

WHAT IT MEANS FOR US

The vast number of possible gene combinations in humans is what makes **genetic fingerprinting** possible. Analyzing just a tiny amount of material from a person's body, such as a drop of blood, is enough to distinguish them from any other person. This technique can be used to identify people who have died in natural disasters, allowing people to know what has happened to friends or family members who have gone missing.

Cheetahs have very little genetic variety. The present-day cheetah population is thought to be descended from only a small number of ancestors.

Variation and Environment

Genes obviously play a major role in determining how an **organism** looks, but they are not the only factor. The **environment** has a part to play, too.

Genotype and phenotype

As we have seen, the information held in a living thing's genes make up its **genotype**. The genotype is the set of instructions for making and maintaining a living thing. Until the instructions are followed, there is no living thing to see.

The actual appearance of the organism produced by following the instructions in the genotype is called its **phenotype**. The phenotype is the physical appearance of the organism—everything that makes it up. If you think of the genotype as being like the blueprint for a building, then the phenotype is the actual place you can walk into.

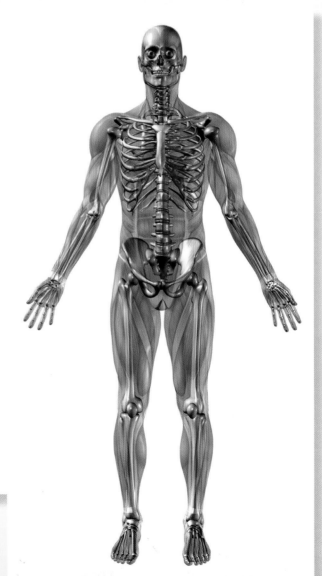

Environmental factors are important in the way the phenotype is built from the genotype. It is important to have instructions to make a tall plant, for example, but if there is a shortage of water or **nutrients** in the soil, the plant will not grow as tall as it might have with abundant water and food.

Your genotype is the plan for building and running your body. Just how that plan is carried out depends on other factors, such as your diet and the amount of exercise you get.

Changing colors

Many gardeners know of at least one particular way changes in the environment have an effect on the appearance of a plant. The hydrangea is a popular garden shrub with flowers that can be shades of pink and blue. The color of the flowers depends on how acidic the soil is. The flowers are blue in acidic soil conditions, mauve in acidic to neutral soil conditions, and pink in alkaline conditions. So the hydrangea is a good indicator of soil conditions, helping the gardener to decide which other plants will grow well there.

WORD BANK
environment   all of the living and non-living things that surround an organism
phenotype   appearance of an organism resulting from the interaction between its genes and the environment

Were you born that way?

For centuries, people have debated whether genetics or the environment are more important in deciding how and who we are. This is often referred to as the "nature versus **nurture**" debate. For example, are some people more likely to gain weight than others? Or is this something that could happen to anyone who eats an unhealthy diet and doesn't exercise enough—regardless of their genes?

A serious problem

About one third of adults in the United States are obese. Of young people between the ages of 2 and 19, 17 percent (12.5 million) are obese. Being overweight can lead to health problems, such as heart disease, so it is a serious issue.

Genes and obesity

So far, more than 200 genes have been identified that are involved in some way in body weight and in fat storage in the body. One of these is called the FTO gene. However, it is not found in everyone, and it is most common in people of European descent. The people who have this gene are likely to be an average of 4½ to 6½ pounds (2 to 3 kilograms) heavier than those who don't have it, and to be more at risk for becoming **obese**.

However, a person who carries this gene is not necessarily doomed to become obese. We can make choices about our lifestyles that can counteract the effect of the genes.

The mouse on the left has a **mutated** form of a gene that has caused it to gain more weight than the normal mouse on the right.

WHAT IT MEANS FOR US

Although genes can obviously play a part in determining body weight, environmental factors come into play as well. Many people have jobs that involve sitting at a desk all day. Often they drive to and from work, and when they get back home, they may spend the evening sitting in front of the television. The lack of exercise means that they are not using up enough of the energy they get from the food they eat. Their bodies will simply store the excess, and the result is weight gain.

By making a positive choice to eat healthy food, to avoid overeating, and to exercise regularly, most people should be able to control their weight.

This overweight cat's appearance is more likely to be the result of too much food and too little exercise, rather than genetics.

Mutations

Because of the huge number of different ways genes can combine from one generation to the next, there would seem to be almost endless possibilities for variation. But this is just shuffling the genetic pack of cards to make new combinations of genes that already exist. We need to be able to explain why sometimes variations appear that have never been seen before.

When a cell divides, its genes are copied so each new cell has a complete set of genes. Every once in a while, a mistake might be made when this copying is done, and a gene will be produced that is different. These changed genes are called **mutations**. In addition to random copying errors, mutations can also be caused by environmental factors, such as radiation and chemicals.

Most mutations are harmful. They interfere with the proper functions of the cell, and, as a result, the cell may die. Sometimes a mutated cell survives, and only because it is one among billions in the body, it has no obvious effect on the rest of the **organism**.

A mutation has made legs grow where this fruit fly's antennae should be.

To the next generation

Mutations that happen in egg or sperm cells affect the whole organism because they will be copied into every one of its cells as it develops. The mutation might have no effect at all; or it might have such a small effect that it causes no advantage or disadvantage. Mutations that result in the death of the organism are called lethals.

A few mutations can be of real benefit to an organism. For example, some mutations can give insects the ability to resist the effects of insecticides. Insects with this mutation are the ones that will survive and reproduce, which means growing populations of insects that are harder to control.

WHAT IT MEANS FOR US

MRSA (yellow in image below) is a type of bacteria that has become very hard to treat. It can cause serious infections, particularly in people who are already unwell, which can create a major problem in hospitals. MRSA was the result of some bacteria having a mutation that then made them resistant to the **antibiotics** used to treat them.

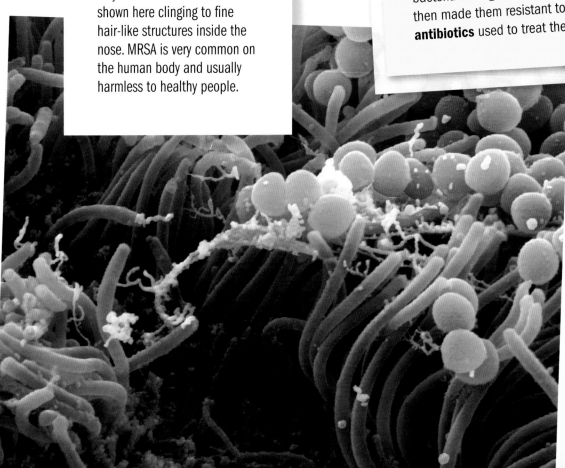

Tiny round MRSA bacteria are shown here clinging to fine hair-like structures inside the nose. MRSA is very common on the human body and usually harmless to healthy people.

Variation and Evolution

The random variations that result from **mutations** are an important part of the way **species** change and adapt over time. Mutations introduce new variety into a species. Although often these changes will be harmful, sometimes they will give the species more chances to survive in changing conditions.

The fight for survival

No matter how successful an **organism** is, it is still going to face challenges to its survival. Being too successful can cause problems if the organism runs out of room to grow or runs out of food to eat. The members of the species might find themselves in competition for the resources needed to survive.

We have already seen how the members of a species are all very similar genetically, but that there is also variety in their **genes** that results in a range of characteristics. The organisms that are best equipped to survive in their **environment** are the ones most likely to reproduce. They will pass their genes to their offspring, making them better equipped to survive, too.

Natural selection

The process by which genes that give an organism an advantage are selected over those that don't is called natural selection. It is an idea that was first put forward by British naturalist Charles Darwin, and independently by Alfred Russel Wallace, in the 19th century.

This statue of Charles Darwin is in the Natural History Museum, in London.

Both men realized that every living thing is in competition for resources. Within a species, there is a wide diversity of individuals, and this is what gives the species the potential to **evolve**. Some individuals will have advantages over others and will be more likely to reproduce. However small the advantage might be, over time it will be selected in favor of less advantageous characteristics in the species.

Natural selection comes about as a result of variation and environmental pressures. The organisms most adapted, or adjusted, to their environment become more numerous than those that aren't. This is sometimes called the "survival of the fittest."

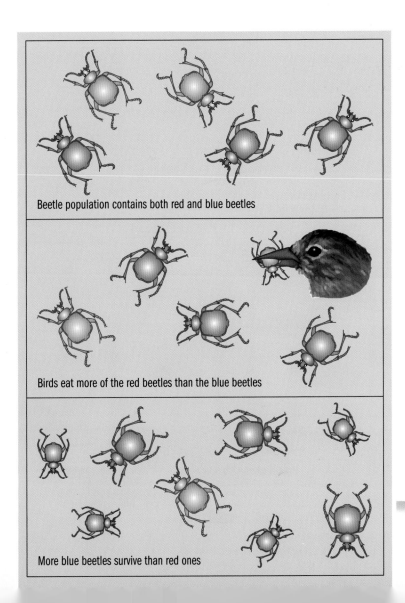

Beetle population contains both red and blue beetles

Birds eat more of the red beetles than the blue beetles

More blue beetles survive than red ones

In this simple example of natural selection at work, there are two similar species of beetle—one red and one blue. If birds find red beetles tastier or easier to catch than blue beetles, then over time there will be many more blue beetles than red ones. In other words, natural selection favors blue beetles.

Adaptations

The features that arise through natural selection and evolution are called **adaptations**. An adaptation is something that gives a living thing an advantage in its environment. For example, the gills of a fish are adaptations that allow it to breathe in water, and the long tongue of a butterfly lets it get nectar from deep inside a flower.

New species

When Darwin was a young man, he traveled to the Galapagos Islands in the Pacific Ocean. There he discovered what has become one of the most famous examples of the way new species appear.

There are several species of finch on the Galapagos Islands. They are all similar but each has a particular adaptation. For example, one has a slender bill that is good for probing for insects, while another has a strong bill that is good for cracking seeds. All of these different species started out as a single species that arrived on the Galapagos from the mainland. However, there were no other birds on the islands to compete with them.

Natural variation within the ancestor of the Galapagos finches eventually gave rise to all of the different species found on the islands today, as the birds made use of the variety of foods available to them.

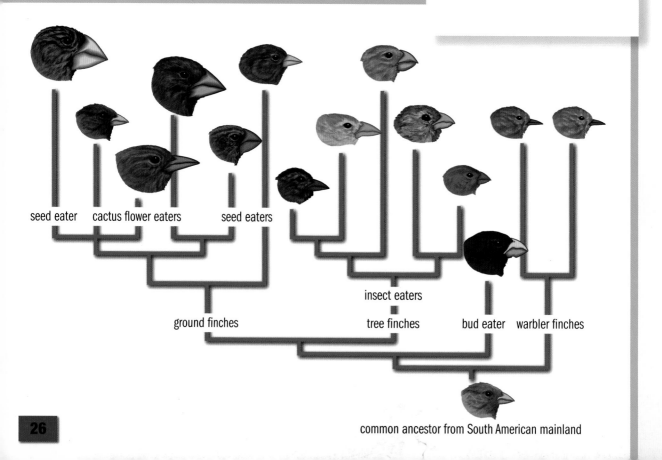

seed eater   cactus flower eaters   seed eaters

ground finches

insect eaters

tree finches   bud eater   warbler finches

common ancestor from South American mainland

Over time, the birds became more specialized and adapted to different types of food. Variation within the original species meant that some birds developed slightly longer and more slender bills and others had slightly thicker and heavier bills. Eventually the different types became so different from the original ancestor birds that they no longer bred with each other. They became new, separate species.

The end of the line

No species lasts forever. One species inevitably gives way to another that is better adapted to changing environmental conditions. A species can become so highly specialized that it no longer has the range of variations needed to adapt. The moist skin of amphibians is an adaptation that allows them to absorb oxygen both in and out of the water. But it also makes them very vulnerable to harmful pollution in the air and in the water. The vast majority of these amphibian species are now **extinct**.

Newly hatched leatherback turtles have to reach the safety of the ocean before predators, such as seabirds, eat them. Only the strongest will survive.

WORD BANK
adaptation feature of a living thing that makes it suited to its environment
extinct describing a species that no longer exists after the last member of the species has died

Cuckoo in the Nest

The common cuckoo of Europe is an unusual kind of bird. It does not build a nest of its own. Instead, it lays its eggs in the nests of other birds. By doing this, it also demonstrates an unusual kind of **discontinuous variation**. To avoid detection, the cuckoo lays an egg that **mimics** the coloring of the unwitting host bird's eggs.

Matching pairs

There is a type of discontinuous variation among female cuckoos that is not apparent until they lay their eggs. Each different type of female cuckoo is matched up to a particular host bird and will only lay eggs that mimic the eggs of that bird. For example, a cuckoo that lays its eggs in a reed warbler's nest will produce eggs that look like the reed warbler's eggs; and a cuckoo that lays eggs in a meadow pipit's nest will have eggs that look like those of the meadow pipit. The "reed warbler" cuckoo cannot switch to being a "meadow pipit" cuckoo.

The cuckoo's egg is larger than the reed warbler's, but the markings are similar enough to fool the reed warblers.

Survival tactics

When the cuckoo chick hatches, it immediately gets to work pushing the host bird's eggs, or any chicks that have hatched, out of the nest. Once it has the nest to itself, it tricks its foster parents into feeding it. The cuckoo chick has an extraordinary begging call, described as sounding like "a whole brood of hungry chicks." The host birds respond to this by working hard to feed the one cuckoo chick.

From mother to daughter

A female cuckoo chick successfully raised in a reed warbler's nest will grow up to be a reed warbler specialist, like its mother. The **genes** that determine the type of eggs laid by the cuckoo are only passed down the female line. The female can breed with any male cuckoo, and this will have no effect on the type of eggs she lays.

Stopping the cuckoo

Some birds have **evolved** strategies to stop the cuckoo. The male reed warbler guards the nest when his mate begins laying her eggs. If the cuckoo does manage to lay an egg in the nest, the reed warblers are more likely to reject it if they have seen the cuckoo nearby.

The cuckoo chick soon grows to be bigger than the reed warblers that feed it.

CASE STUDY

Blood Groups

Humans are divided into different blood groups—another type of **discontinuous variation**.

ABO blood group

The most common of the blood groups is called the ABO group. It can be divided into A, B, AB, and O blood types. The different types refer to differences between each person's red blood **cells**. A person can only be one particular type. It is not possible to be a mixture of different types.

Blood transfusions

Hospitals keep supplies of blood for use during surgery or to replace blood lost by accident victims. Blood for transfusions is stored in places called blood banks. The blood can only be kept for a short time and so supplies must be replenished, or restored, all of the time—and so volunteer donors are vital.

Blood bags are carefully labeled. Giving the wrong type of blood to someone could be disastrous.

A person can't be given just anyone's blood. Before a blood transfusion can be given to someone, their blood type has to be determined. If the wrong type of blood is given, the body's immune system will attack the new blood cells and destroy them. This means, for example, that a person with type A blood can only receive blood from a type A donor.

The rhesus factor

In addition to the ABO types, there is also the **rhesus (Rh) factor**. There are two Rh blood groups. A person can be either type Rh positive or type Rh negative. This refers to the presence or absence of features on the red blood cells. Someone with blood type O, who is also Rh negative, is referred to as being "O negative."

This chart shows how complex it is to match blood donors to recipients. Many factors need to be considered. Plasma is the liquid that blood cells are found in.

Blood type of recipient	Donor		
	Whole blood	Red cells	Plasma
O+	O+ or O-	O+ or O-	O+, O-, A+, A-, B+, B-, AB+, or AB-
O-	O-	O-	O+, O-, A+, A-, B+, B-, AB+, or AB-
A+	A+ or A-	O+, O-, A+, or A-,	A+, A-, AB+, or AB-
A-	A-	A- or O-	A+, A-, AB+, or AB-
B+	B+ or B-	O+, O-, B+, or B-	B+, B-, AB+, or AB-
B-	B-	O- or B-	B+, B-, AB+, or AB-
AB+	AB+ or AB-	O+, O-, A+, A-, B+, B-, AB+, or AB-	AB+ or AB-
AB-	AB -	O-, A-, B-, or AB-	AB+ or AB-

WHAT IT MEANS FOR US

People with type O blood are sometimes referred to as universal donors. The reason for this is that they can safely donate blood to anyone in the ABO group. However, they themselves can only receive blood from type O donors. People who are AB, on the other hand, can receive blood from people of any type.

WORD BANK

rhesus (Rh) factor feature of red blood cells that may be present in some people (rhesus positive) and

Insect Societies

Some insects, such as termites, ants, and some types of wasps and bees, live together in large colonies. These insects are referred to as social insects because they form large societies of many individuals divided into different types, each with a task to perform.

Castes

There are generally three types, or castes, of insect within a colony. These are queens, workers, and males. Some workers may be larger than the others. They are the colony's soldiers, and their job is to defend it against attack from threats, such as insects from different colonies. All of the workers are females.

New colonies

Once a year the insect colony produces a new generation of queens and males. Worker ants and termites are wingless; it is only the new queens and the males that can fly. They leave the colony to mate with ants from other colonies. After mating, the males die—their only job within the colony is completed. The queen looks for a suitable place to lay her eggs, and so begins a new colony.

Nature and nurture again

Whether an ant becomes a queen or a worker is determined by its **genes** and by the **environment**. Researchers studied the Florida harvester ant and discovered that the descendants of some males were more likely to become queens, while those of other males were more likely to be workers.

The researchers also investigated the role played by the ants' diet. It appeared that the ant **larvae** that became queens had a diet made up of other animals, while the worker ants had a more plant-based diet. So, both nature (in the form of the ant's genes) and **nurture** (in the form of diet) play a part. Exactly how the two work together is not certain.

Megacolony

Social insects, such as ants and bees, will attack intruders from other colonies. Scientists recently discovered a vast megacolony of Argentine ants that stretches around the world. Originating in South America, the ants have been carried unknowingly from continent to continent by humans. One supercolony of ants is believed to extend 3,700 miles around the Mediterranean coast of Europe. Ants from the European supercolony introduced to ants from the Japan supercolony won't fight, proving that they are related.

Worker ants escort winged males from the nest.

Artificial Variation

Throughout history, humans have looked for ways to introduce new varieties into living things. For example, we have selected crops that are pest-resistant and give high yields, and then we plant them instead of the less hardy or less productive plants.

Selective breeding

Selective breeding, or artificial selection, is the process of deliberately breeding plants and animals to produce offspring with characteristics that we find useful. For example, farmers want to have cows that yield the most milk, or chickens that lay the most eggs. By continually selecting and breeding from only the individuals that produce the most milk or eggs, there will eventually be new varieties of a **species** that have the characteristics we want.

A variety, also called a **breed**, will have characteristics that set it apart—but it is not a new species. Any variety of a species can breed with any other variety. There are a great many cattle breeds, such as the Holstein cow, which is a good milk producer, and the Aberdeen Angus, which is prized for the quality of its beef.

Plant breeders have grown many different varieties of pepper, from sweet bell peppers to hot chilis. All of them belong to the same species.

The gene pool

A **gene** pool is all of the genes present within a species—not just the genes found in a single individual. The greater the variety of genes within the species, the more adaptable it is likely to be. By breeding plants and animals to have certain characteristics, we are reducing the size of their gene pool by rejecting the features we don't want.

For thousands of years, people have kept and raised pigs. There are now more than 300 breeds. However, wild boars like this one were the ancestors of all our domestic pigs.

From wolf to dog

One of the most startling examples of people producing new breeds within a single species is the huge variety of shapes, sizes, and characteristics we see in domestic, or pet, dogs. From tiny chihuahuas to large and powerful mastiffs, all of these animals belong to a single species—and all of the differences between them are a result of selective breeding.

The wolves in our homes

It has long been thought that dogs are descended from wolves, but it is only in recent years that scientists have been able to prove this. Researchers compared the **genomes** of dogs and grey wolves, and discovered a difference of only 0.2 percent. This shows there is a very close link between the two animals.

These wild wolves are very closely related to the dogs that share many of our homes.

The origins of the dog

The best guess at the moment when dogs were first domesticated is around 15,000 years ago. Where this took place is also uncertain. There is some evidence to suggest it happened in East Asia, but it also seems likely that some breeds of dog started out in the Middle East and Africa. The best explanation is that wolves were domesticated in several different places at around the same time.

The modern dog

Most of the dog breeds we are familiar with today have been developed over the last 200 years by breeders, and they have carefully selected dogs with the desired characteristics. Careful records, called pedigrees, are kept of breeding to ensure that the character of the dog is maintained.

The German shepherd dog, for example, originated from mountain sheepdogs that were bred by Captain Max von Stephanitz at the end of the 19th century. He selected dogs, to work as herding dogs, that were strong and intelligent. The German shepherd became popular as a working dog for a number of activities, including police work.

It may be hard to imagine that the wide variety of domestic, or pet, dogs are all descended from wolves, but they are.

Genetic engineering

While we can use selective breeding to change the characteristics of plants and animals over generations, **genetic engineering** allows us to change them in a single step. And whereas selective breeding is only carried out within a species, with genetic engineering we can take genes from one species and add them to another.

This ram has been genetically engineered to produce genes that can be used to treat human genetic illnesses.

Designer plants

Plants can be genetically engineered to be resistant to powerful chemicals that are used to kill weeds. Genetically modified (GM) soy beans were one of the first crops to be modified in this way. In 1994 the first GM plant to be approved for human consumption was a tomato that had been genetically altered to ripen more slowly. This increased the amount of time the tomatoes could stay on the supermarket shelf.

Another plant developed by genetic engineering was golden rice. A carrot gene was inserted into the rice plant so that it would produce more vitamin A. The idea behind this was that people's diets could be improved by eating the golden rice.

Questions to think about

Many people welcomed the development of golden rice and its higher vitamin A content. Around 400 million people worldwide suffer from vitamin A deficiency in their diet. It is a problem in large areas of Africa, India, and elsewhere in Asia. The **World Health Organization** estimates that 500,000 children each year go blind because of lack of vitamin A.

However, environmental campaigners have fought against the introduction of golden rice. One argument against it is that it will have an effect on the variety of food crops that are grown. If people rely on the golden rice, they might no longer grow other plants, leading to a loss of **biodiversity**. What do you think of these two opposing views?

WHAT IT MEANS FOR US

Human genes have also been used in genetic engineering. Cystic fibrosis is a common genetic disease that attacks the lungs and digestive system. It is an incurable condition caused by a faulty gene that fails to produce a **protein** that the body needs. By inserting a good copy of the gene into sheep, they can be made to produce the missing protein in their milk. This can then be extracted and used to treat the cystic fibrosis sufferer.

Consultant surgeon James Bainbridge headed a team at Moorfields Eye Hospital, London, successfully treating an **inherited** eye condition using gene therapy.

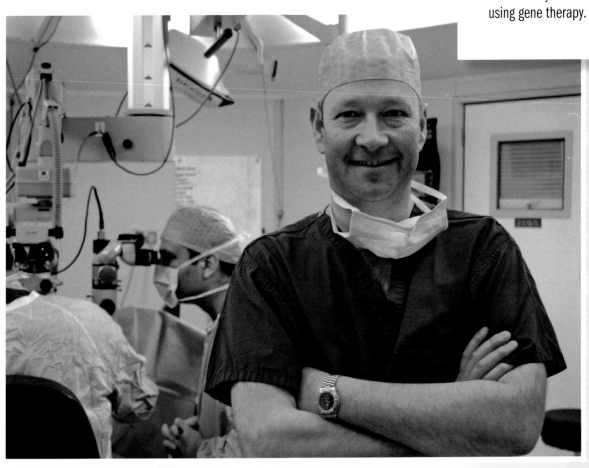

Clones

Clones are organisms that are genetically identical. Any differences between one clone and another is the result of environmental factors. There are many examples of clones in nature. Strawberry plants that grow from runners, rather than seeds, are genetically identical to the parent plant. Gardeners and plant breeders will often produce new plants by taking cuttings from a plant. The plants that grow from the cuttings are clones of the original plant.

A strawberry plant spreads by producing offshoots called runners. The new plant is genetically identical to the parent.

WHAT IT MEANS FOR US

One possibility for the use of cloned animals is in the mass production of animals engineered to carry human genes, such as the sheep used in the treatment of cystic fibrosis. Another possibility is the creation of genetically modified pigs that could produce organs suitable for human transplants.

Clone research

In 1997, researchers in Scotland successfully produced the world's first cloned mammal, an event that would never happen in nature. This was Dolly the sheep. Scientists cloned Dolly by taking the genetic material from a donor sheep cell and inserting it into another cell from which the genetic material had been removed. The new cell was made to begin dividing in the laboratory. When it was successfully growing, it was implanted into the womb of a female sheep where it continued to develop until birth.

The problems with cloning

Cloning of animals is difficult and expensive to achieve. Over 90 percent of attempts fail to produce offspring that survive. Research has shown also that those that do survive may have poor health and die early for mysterious reasons. Scientists suspect that part of the reason may be that the cloned animal's genes are not working properly.

Cloning and variation

Another disadvantage to cloning is that it works against variation. To clone a whole herd of cows with especially high milk yields might, at first, seem like a good idea; however, there would be huge risks. Cloning reduces the gene pool to its minimum. All of the animals in the cloned herd would be identical, with identical immune systems. If the herd were struck by disease, either all of them would live—or all of them would die.

There is no doubt that there is a place for artificial cloning, but we would be very shortsighted if we were to fail to safeguard the amazing variety in the world.

Common confusions

Cloning and genetic engineering

Although they are often thought of together, cloning is not a form of genetic engineering. When an organism is cloned, the genes of the parent **organism** are not changed in any way. If they were, the offspring would be genetically different from its parent, and, therefore, not a clone.

This cow was the first cloned animal in Latin America. Her calf was born in September 2004, through natural reproduction, and scientists say her growth is normal.

Food Variety

Have you ever wondered about the huge variety of fruit and vegetables that we have to choose from today? Have you noticed all the different types of apples and potatoes? You might not know that the fruit and vegetables we eat today are very different when compared to the ones that were eaten thousands of years ago, when there was much less variety. Growers have produced a huge range of variations in food plants over the centuries.

Potatoes

Did you know that there are around 5,000 varieties of potato worldwide? Three thousand of them are found only in the Andes Mountains of South America, where they were first grown by farmers over 7,000 years ago.

Sweetcorn

The ancestor of sweetcorn, called teosinte, had just five to twelve little **kernels**, each one held inside a hard shell.

Kiwi fruit

The kiwi fruit was originally a hard berry that grew in China. Plant breeders in New Zealand developed the soft green fruit eaten today.

Tomatoes

Tomatoes grown today can weigh a thousand times as much as their wild ancestors, which were small green fruits first grown in South America. Today there are thousands of varieties of tomato, some with amusing names such as Alberto Shatters, Butter 'n' Eggs, Green Zebra, and Little Willie's Mouthful.

Cabbage

All of the varieties of cabbage, brussels sprouts, broccoli, and cauliflower we eat today, were developed from a single wild ancestor—the wild cabbage, or wild mustard plant.

Carrots

Carrots originally came in a wide variety of colors, including red, yellow, and even purple. The orange carrots we are familiar with today were developed in the Netherlands in the seventeenth century.

Wheat

Wheat, a type of grass, was first grown over 10,000 years ago. The first farmers selected mutant varieties that had large grains that were firmly attached to the stalks. The result was the development of a plant that couldn't survive in the wild because it could no longer disperse its seeds.

Eggplant

Eggplant are not just large, oval-shaped, dark-purple vegetables. Many different varieties are grown in parts of Asia. They can be reddish purple, white, yellow, or green. They can be small and round, long and slim, or weigh up to two pounds.

Apples

The wild ancestor of the apple grows in Central Asia. The name of the city of Alma-ata in Kazakhstan means "Grandfather of Apples." Today, more than 7,500 varieties of apple are grown in orchards around the world.

WORD BANK
kernel   single whole grain of a cereal

Glossary

adaptation feature of a living thing that makes it suited to its environment

allele one of a pair of alternative forms of a gene

antibiotic drug used to fight infections caused by bacteria

biodiversity variety of different living things found in a place

breed group of domestic animals with characteristics that distinguish them from other members of the same species

cell basic unit of life; single cells are the simplest form of life. More complex organisms, such as humans, are made up of trillions of cells.

continuous variation variation that takes place over a range of measurements (for example, height and weight)

discontinuous variation variation in which there are only a few distinct varieties, with nothing in between (for example, blood groups)

dominant gene allele that determines the appearance, or phenotype, of the organism. For example, if a person has one hair color allele for brown hair and one for blonde hair, their hair will be brown because brown is the dominant gene.

environment all of the living and non-living things that surround an organism

evolve develop and change over time

extinct describing a species that no longer exists after the last member of the species has died

fertile able to reproduce

fertilization when a sperm cell joins with an egg to make a new cell with two genomes

gene basic unit of heredity in living things, the means by which characteristics are passed from one generation to the next

genetic engineering deliberately changing the genes of an organism in a laboratory

genetic fingerprinting process of using a person's genetic material to identify him or her

genome all of the genetic information held in the cells of an organism

genotype combination of gene pairs (alleles) in an organism with regard to which genes are dominant and which are recessive

heredity transfer of characteristics from parents to their offspring

hybrid organism that is the offspring of parents from two different species

inherit receive from the previous generation

kernel single whole grain of a cereal

larva (plural: **larvae**) juvenile forms of insects; a maggot is a larva of a fly

mimic take on the appearance of something else

mutate undergo a change in the genes of an organism

mutation gene that has undergone change

nurture all the environmental factors that influence the behavior and traits of an organism

nutrient substance that living things need in order to survive and grow

obese so overweight that health is endangered

organism any kind of living thing

phenotype appearance of an organism resulting from the interaction between its genes and the environment

protein one of a group of complex chemicals produced by living things to perform tasks such as breaking down food and building cells

recessive gene gene in which the effects are only seen if both alleles in the gene pair are recessive (for example, the gene for blonde hair)

rhesus (Rh) factor feature of red blood cells that may be present in some people (rhesus positive) and not in others (rhesus negative)

species group of living things that have shared characteristics and which can breed together to produce fertile offspring

subspecies smaller group within a species. A subspecies has some features that set it apart from other members of the species, but it is not sufficiently different to be considered as a species in its own right.

World Health Organization (WHO) branch of the United Nations that is responsible for dealing with health issues around the world

Find Out More

Books

Bright, Michael. *The Diversity of Species* (Timeline: Life on Earth). Chicago, IL: Heinemann Library, 2009.

Crosby, Jeff and Sherly Ann Jackson. *Little Lions, Bull Baiters, and Hunting Hounds: A History of Dog Breeds*. Plattsburgh, NY: Tundra Books, 2008.

Farndon, John. *From DNA to GM Wheat* (Chain Reactions series). Chicago, IL: Heinemann Library, 2007.

Nardo, Don. *The Theory of Evolution: A History of Life on Earth*. Mankato, MN: Compass Point Books, 2010.

Rand, Casey. *DNA and Heredity* (Investigating Cells series). Chicago, IL: Heinemann Library, 2011.

Rand, Casey. *Classification of Animals* (Sci-Hi: Life Science series). Chicago, IL: Raintree, 2009.

Vaughan, Jenny. *Genetics* (Science in the News). Mankato, MN: Smart Apple Media, 2010.

Websites

learn.genetics.utah.edu
Learn Genetics: This is a wonderfully detailed and comprehensive site with information on genes, heredity, variation, how cells work, and much more.

evolution.berkeley.edu/evolibrary/home.php
Understanding Evolution: Described as "your one-stop source for information on evolution," it is an excellent summary of ideas on how evolution works.

e360.yale.edu/feature/arctic_roamers_the_move_of_southern_species_into_far_north/2370/
This website has information about grolar bears and other hybrids.

www.nature.com/scitable/topicpage/gregor-mendel-and-the-principles-of-inheritance-593
Find out about Gregor Mendel and his discoveries concerning inheritance on this website.

www.aboutdarwin.com
Learn more about the life and work of naturalist Charles Darwin on this website.

www.blood.co.uk/about-blood/blood-group-basics
This website has more information about blood groups. It also describes what happens when someone becomes a blood donor.

Topics to research

Dinovariation

What do we know about variation in living things that lived a long time ago, such as the different types of dinosaurs? They are no longer around, so we can't observe them to find out if some ran faster than others, or if some had better camouflage, for example. Did natural selection and adaptation benefit dinosaurs and other prehistoric living things, just as it has benefitted the plants and animals around us today?

Here are a couple of places you might start looking for answers:

paleobiology.si.edu/dinosaurs/index.html

www.mnh.si.edu/exhibits/darwin/carrano.html

Classroom characteristics

How many different ways can you think of to describe how the people in your school show variations between each other?

Index